That We Too

Free May Live

By Dudley (CHRIS) Christian

A

Pause For Poetry ©

Publication

Acknowledgement:

Special thanks to my wife, Marilyn Christian for compiling, organizing and finalizing the books of my collections. Her photographing and editing skills were vital to all of my works.

ISBN:978-0-9916853-4-9

First Edition December 2012
Revised Edition June 2017

Graphic Cover was designed by Marilyn & Dudley Christian

Dudley (Chris) Christian founded and hosted the first and only *"PAUSE FOR POETRY"* show dedicated solely to the introduction of new and unknown poets and their works. This TV series ran from 1974 to 1985.

<u>An Opening Word by the Author...</u>

Many people often ask:

"How do you write and do you have to often rewrite your material?"

I have long summed up my answer to the above with the following:

"A Word, the written word, small purveyor of a thought, so like a thought, once thought, cannot be recalled, so too, a word once writ, should need NOT be re-written, for with such licence, we would but change ... the very substance of the thought."

... DNC © 1970

Table of Contents

Dear Reader:

Take a time out, pause please, now input slowly...

It's a time to consider, re-think, and contemplate. Look at a "Little Girl in Quiet Sleep" (page 46) . See all the troubles of today are gone. All of yesterday's woes have been corrected and tomorrow is really bright and shiny, as we yet are unaware of their impact on our lives.

Yet "I've Been Reading Past Histories" (page 48) of when too "I Was But a Tiny Babe" (page 50) in someone's arms. Hoping "If You Would But Treat Me Equal" (page 101) or at least give me more than lip-service when I try to explain with "Freedom of Speech" (page 107), that eerie sound made when the "Blood of Innocents Cry" (page 104), of our breaking hearts as we continue trying to grasp "The Will To Live" (page 95) onto that thin life-line which just may show you, or us, "A Grim Recollection" (page 86), and the avenue into the past lives of you and I...

Rejection...

Oh rejection you many headed serpent you

Why strike you out so constantly at

Oh rejection you demon of desperation

You drive my thoughts on to suicide

Life strikes out and I pain do sustain

And reaching in you seem happy only then

To evermore add to my toil and pain

Oh rejection you my handiwork a mockery make

My livelihood like candy from a babe you take

My pleasures you add sorrow to 'til they

But only in distant cold appearance stay

My hands reach out for what is truly mine

You let me touch and promising more withdraw

You dangle hope before these eyes of mine

And as they look thereto remove what li'l they saw

My legal sustenance mine in time of need

Insurance which for years on end I've paid

You hold back tho I scarce can feed

The mouths which depended once on what I made

Rejection you have cut me off midstream

My hopes and plans you have laid askew

My creditors lose confidence in my schemes

And join in ranks alas it seems with you

My taxes which so long have taken been

By Government to assist with others needs

Now this help is by that Government rejected

When from it sustenance for life I plead

Rejection you many headed monster you

You've bent and broken me 'til at last

No pride nor shame I carry more within

No self-respect to fight like in the past

Dejected here in bed each night I lay

My head upon a pillow and bed cold

What left is there for you to take

Me now an outcast from the world

Rejection I for nights on end do wait

With wants... desires... needs all left unfilled

Called only when by others needed yet

Their seldom felt needs but to fulfill

Oh rejection you have had your day

I feel no more desire nor will to try

My heart is like a dam too filled to stay

My soul and life is empty mine eyes dry

I walk about and touch so slight

Each lasting object which life gave

A reminder every one of good times bright

Before you came to lead me to my grave

Alas Rejection take fast now my hand

I at last in full comprehension wait

You but a fore-runner of death are

I lay back now content I in my fate

Laughs... loves... hurts... pains... despair

Depression... anger... sorrow aye and shame

These all you've led me through rejection

Each one a step... a step in your game

Then delay no more your final move

Reach out rejection and Deaths door let jar

Let life itself thy final rejection show

Remove my now useless carcass off afar

Oh rejection you many headed serpent you

These many years your best plans foiled did I

But will has left me now... let enter peace

Contented bliss mine at last... even as I die...

Thru-out the world we the non-whites
are all brothers thru
their hate-filled actions towards us

Marriage: A Die In Institution

When God created woman

Mans helpmate to be

He placed them in a garden

To live love and be free

Then came a time of sorrow

When outnumbered man did grow

So to protect her vested interest

Woman to the Lord did go

"Oh Lord" she said a-weeping

"Once each a man we had

Who stayed long by our sides

Thru good times and thru bad

But times Lord been a-changing

'Til now in grief we find

For each woman to be happy

We need share Lord the man of mine

And I dear Lord am fearful

For what if perchance he lie

With some younger prettier woman

Oh Lord who's better there than I

So good Lord please consider

And try to ease our plight

You know oh Lord it's hard for us

To please him each and every night."

Now the Lord took the petition

Devised he did a plan

Where man would be bound to woman

Where woman could keep her man

For a while this seemed to work out

'Til woman felt so secure

She added bits and pieces   .

For she ruled the man now sure

She lay the rules for loving

The time the place the day

The ways she felt was perfect

His options she cast away

His needs were placed as second

For she must come first she cried

Her moods and angers governed

No matter how hard he tried

She'd bear him yet his children

If it fit into her plans

Or destroy them while yet fetus

Consent unasked of any man

She'd be a wife and lover

Stay at home while hard he toiled

Nag him if he failed at working

His pleasures constantly foil

Yet if he thought of leaving

She'd so sweetly to him say

"Leave, but the house and kids are mine

The car and half your pay

For we have got a contract

Which says you're mine for life

To stay, protect, provide and keep

Secured for I'm your wife

No longer can you gad about

For you man belong to me

By God... by laws... forevermore

Protected I by matrimony

And if you seek another

Whom with my place to fill

I'll take you to the cleaners

So it's best you do my will

For I will never embarrassed be

Without my full vengeance due

My security insurance marriage is

The underwriter love is you..."

Thus was it that Gods marriage plan

An institution came to be

A life prison term for many men

No escape nor parole to see

No time off for behaviour good

No outside games to play

Just quiet constant servitude

Passive solitude everyday

And woman was elated

For she now held it seemed

A means her love life to secure

Controlled ever by her schemes

For could she not now govern

Her man thruout his life

While he must wait in gratitude

For favours few from his wife

So once again woman triumphed

O'er e'en Gods best laid plan

Like the apple in the garden

Man once more can't understand

So he in deep petition

Did to the good Lord go

To ask for help and guidance

'Gainst the woes he'd come to know

But sitting with their lawyers

The Lord who no lie can tell

Admitted of the loopholes in

The plan fashioned so well

Gave He man this consolation

"Your days here I'll decrease

That tho your contract carries

Early death will give release

And for each year you suffer

I equal will retract

One year of life Earth upon

To hasten your coming back

But should you fail your contract

I'll add misery to your life

To your Mistress I'll send a lover

Who of her will tell your wife

Or else another man shall know

Your pleasures and joys of home

While you cuckold must do without

Yet provide her still a home

For these things I her promised

When I devised the marriage plan

My wife says I must honor them

The same forever for each man"

At last man gained understanding

That this way it must be

Once bound to wife by marriage

No way freedom again he to see

So Man in silent submission

Told the Lord he'd do His bid

Walked the long walk to the altar

Muttering low... "I will... I will... I will..."

There is no shame

in having been conquered

and no pride in having

had others held in slavery

Despair...

Alas and now I find

I have not house nor money

Neither charges aye nor favours

For sore despair it seems

To ride upon my back

My shoulders stoop they low

Beneath the load

Placed on them by you oh World

My mind in dismal reaches

Of depression play

My laughing soul no longer

Laughs aloud

My joking lips these days

In solemn silence stay

Alas oh life what have I

What have I now e'er but myself

My self own useless hulk of flesh

My pride-less pride

My un-respectful self-respect

These cannot now in any way fulfill

These cannot warm my bed

Nor clad my back

Nor even yet can these my hungers kill

Like a poor and wretched pauper I

I shuffle thru the leaves of City Park

In search am I an empty bench

To pause and rest upon

A paper old by days

Its news of wretched World around

This shall now to me a blanket be

Alas oh wretch I am

Once walking proud with man

Once fed and full of love and mirth

Once happy and respected by

Those thru whom to others I gave birth

Now World oh wretched cold

And unforgiving World

You have it seemed upon my face

Your back turned

You have revolved and stopped

So short of me

To turmoil fill my life

With my every breath

Oh wretch in life I must remain

Uncontent yet cannot ease my pains

For World when from me

You did yourself displace

Even death itself it seems

With you you took

No solace now I find in suicide

For pain and injury alone

Will I endure

Yet life of sorts will linger on

And on and on

Alas and now I find

I have not house nor friend

Nor home

Nor money

Neither charges aye nor favours

For sore depression seems to ride

Upon my back

Seems to ride

So high upon my back...

> If more wives shared sex
>
> instead of just giving sex
>
> less men would seek sex elsewhere

To Be Words Of Lust Or Woe

To be words of lust or woe

'Tis but a warm and feeling good

Appearing when you by I go

And far away and pure and chaste

My love will long for you grow

For in years to come you may seek to find

A distant love which does so silently grow

> May the cup of life overflow its wealth and health
>
> into your lap giving you the very best

Where Goest Thou Oh Wandering Heart

Where goest thou oh wandering heart
Once more apart from me
To seek shelter elsewhere in life
My aches, pains and grief to free
What reason gave I unto you
Once more from me to go
No reason shall save emptiness
Since last, love lost, I know
Oh wandering heart you like myself
Traverse the earth in search of love
Without a moment long fulfilled
In peace sent from above
Ah, yes shell, a man you are
Or at least so to all you seem
Save to my thoughts which clearly see
Into your false world of dreams
And as you sit there lonely yet
You hear me race and beat and break
Still in your stubborn attitude
No chance for love in life you take
You sit and moan you lay and think
Of pasts that you once lived
Then return deep into yourself

My needs, wants and hopes unfilled
So shall I leave to seek refuge
Wherein I again can frolic play
A casing which life lives within
Through happy night or lonely day
Wait heart return you wanderer
Beat long within my breast
I've seen your reason and regret
My self-pity and selfishness
Give me a chance again to be
The happy loving being you knew
A chance to find another love
Who to us both will prove true.
Oh wandering heart here you belong
Here where so long you've beat
You can't forsake this wanderer
Whom life so oft ill-treat
Oh shell you wanderer so like I
Let me beat warm in thy breast
'Til life smiles long upon us both
Or sweet welcome death gives rest.

Media is never prejudiced they merely give
only their opinion or side of a story

There Are Things In Life

Tho we each must face life's trials

As we travel on our way

There are measures -- which we all should stand upon

There are things in life we treasure

They're the things which show our worth

They're the little rights of freedom

That are ours as men from birth

Each and every one must measure

Their desires hopes and plans

But before them all -- we must stand fast

We must stand fast on the measures of a man

For a man is often measured

By his money wealth in store

Or again at times by places

Or position he may hold

But throughout the ages past

It's been proven through life's plan

That no-conformity, no-compromise

Is the measure of a man

Yes the measure of full happiness

Is contentment in our life

And for peace and joy we find

We must bear the bitter strife

So we all must 'valuate ourselves

Forming in our minds a plan

That no-conformity no-compromise

Is life's true measure of a man

Watch the travelling public like lemmings

following to destruction

the media's concept of what to do

with any given day

Lifesaving Ladders

Light, cleared and swung out

Area, cleared of rails etc.

Davits, manned

Drop, ladder over side

Employ, personnel

Raft, lifted up, out and placed

Secure, swing outboard

Idi Amin should be bleached white like his teachers for his actions have him that honour earned

Dearest Darling This Is Not Goodbye

Dearest Darling this is not goodbye

The Heart a lonely hunter rests

For but a while then again will try

Each season of life it careful fills

With hopes, joys, wants and pain

Yet after all the aches have gone

The hopes and joys remain

Like a dry and dusty desert street

We walk -- feeling stifled by the dust

Our lives in turmoil so oft has been

We know no longer who to trust

In soul and mind we reach e'er out

For from life's sinking sand a hand

A grip to grasp firm and secure

Firmer ground whereon to stand

In silent pleas we ask for help

Reassurance and understanding

For someone who so like ourselves

Can appreciate our hearts undertakings

An open book we pages like

Lay bare to the World our souls

Seeking but therefrom one reader who

Will comprehend the truth it holds

Alas life looks the heart once at

Like a lonely hunter -- lost -- forlorn

And holds no pity for its shell

But whispers to it just "Go On"

So on we go as life did demand

A cold -- empty -- hollow shell

Our filling, living, loving heart

Listening on to Love's death knell

The circle of love has been displaced

By the hands so cruel of fate

To make for us a triangle which

We in must silently wait

And you and I nor we nor they

Any way can speed the ending

Nor can we see out beyond today

And the chosen moment we're spending

So dearest this is not goodbye

No time our tears to let flow

Tis but a reprieve for our hearts.

Better each to get to true know

In time pre'aps long or maybe short

Our paths again they'll cross

We'll meet anew in seasons bright

Full forgetful of our loss

And like the clinging rose's vine

We then deep knit shall blend

Our hearts in loves unison renewed

Wherein we'll know no more pretend

Then outside hikers you and I

Shall walk long alone life's way

Our hearts no longer lonely hunters then

No more obstacles in our way

But guiding lights both shining bright

Each other life's paths we'll show

'Til our lost -- cold -- lonely -- empty shell

We in love ne'er again shall know

Dearest Darling this is not Goodbye

The heart a lonely hunter rests

For but awhile then again will try

For but awhile then again will try.

Speak Not To Me Of Exploits Past...

Speak not to me of exploits past

Nor of husbands you have known

Speak not to me of loves you've owned

For I too have had my own

Give not to me your aches that be

Your hurts and pains of bygone years

Give me instead your feelings welcome warm

Your arms outstretched to ease my tears

Speak not to me of hurts you've felt

When cast you down have been

Like you with man I cast down too

Have been with lady friend

Ask not of me to tell to you

My woes and aches gone by

Waste not the time we have to spend

Precious time for you and I

Speak not to me of what could have been

With you and someone else

But speak to me instead of plans

For you and for myself

Speak to me gently and of love

Of cares which ne'er will die

Speak soft to me of loves own ways

Which now we two can try

Speak not to me of bygone years

Of wasted hours spent

Ask not of me of those I knew

Nor of those whom I feel repent

Speak just to me of love, of love

Of love, of love and life

Speak sweet to me of truth and warmth

And of how our NOW is alright

Speak now to me of now

Speak not of yesterday

For it is gone and in its stead

There remains but now... today

Speak not to me tomorrow of

For it we may ne'er see

But today... tonight we full can find

In love our fondest dreams

And as the morning breaks upon

And casts our eyes once more

We two can look this world upon

Or enter its dark doors

We then can look and say that we

Have lived and loved and been

We two alone will know we are

Much more than just good friend

Speak not to me of bygone days

Speak not of hurts and aches and pains

Speak not of those who caused them to

Fall once your life upon in shame

Speak not to me of times that've been

Cause not me these to recall

I want your arms around me warm

To help us each forget them all

I want your lips your love so warm

To help us each forget them all...

The major trouble with all divorces is usually
only in the minds of the children involved

Ah But Madame Monsieur Would You?

How long would you remain content
To see your hopes and plans
Be taken all and shredded down
Replaced by another man's
How long in silence would you sit
Whilst all your work and pain
Went naught for every time someone
Changed once their minds again
How long would you endure insecure
When deep within 'twas plain
That fate 'n' destiny could be yours
Madame, Monsieur how long would you
How long would you remain?

I am but a Spirit free
With love and warmth full score
Seeking but to live unashamed
Of that which I endure
My hopes have all been shattered
My dreams all fade away
How long then Madame Monsieur
Must I go on this way?

I like a lover married am

To one who should be my own

But find my love another has

Who disrupts my happy home

I cannot speak out clearly

For my love would me despise

I walk alone or by his side

Bent head and cast down eyes

In private I entreat my love

Smile on me for love's sake

But ridicule I receive back

My pleas he doth not take

I find the home which we have built

He in her name has placed

Am I to live on still herein

My everything disgraced

He says 'tis better yet this way

Than for us to separate be

Madame, Monsieur how long would you

Endure if you were me?

Or maybe like a husband I

Who loves his wife and home

Yet watches others successfully try

To make his wife their own

And in silence must I remain
Cuckold in truth each day
While in another's arms my wife
In sensuous pleasures lay
Her lover cares not that I be
But walks with her besides
A smirk upon his face doth play
As they cross where I do lie
In splendour everyday she clad
Him, with garments grand
And speaks to me in sarcasm
About her lover man
I go to law myself to free
But am told my marriage stands
Madame Monsieur if it was you
Would you live on like this man?

Again as a mother old and grey
Who's borne the pains of time
To bring to maturity good and true
The offsprings of her time
Now sits she in a welfare home
Alone, unloved, afraid, unseen
With naught but hand out sustenance
She who gave them her everything

And placed within her lovely home
Where as children they she raised
The person stands who cast her out
To whom her children now give praise
No longer is she mother called
E'en that title now is gone
Worn by one who knew no pain
Of the young ones by her borne
Yet she can roll a wedding ring
For her church says she must stay
Madame Monsieur what marriage this
Would you still within it stay?

Oh Dad oh Dad oh Father old
Tell of your younger days
When proud you walked 'mong mankind
As men spoke your name in praise
When you did fight full equal free
Besides one who now fills your place
Content within the home you built
While your name's in low disgrace
Your wife who took your livelihood
And drained your strength of life
Her favours now visits him upon
Yet still remains your wife

Until the grave shall set you free
You're bound for so law stands
No divorce, annulment separation
No rights to make new plans
No voice within the walls you built
Nothing but just what you're told
Madame Monsieur if this was you
How long could you endure?

I am that woman and that man
That mother father too
I built and borne and sacrificed
To be free to live like you
I've set my goals so like your own
And watched you them cast down
I've seen my pride and my respect
Trampled by you 'neath the ground
I've quiet keep as you usurped
The place I helped to build
I've been proud of my home simple
'Til this pride you sought to kill
I've let you have all that I own
In return for favours few
Yet tho so meager what I ask
It was oft refused by you

At last I feel a prisoner here
And I say now set me free
Madame Monsieur I can't live with you
I must have a destiny.

What for I want you question me
What seek I out to find
What love now new can I embrace
What knowledge or strength of mind
What house new can I construct
What jobs can I create
What employ outside these walls there be
If you let me separate
These questions all so shallow lie
As you your ways defend
We could not live as lovers one
We maybe could live as friend
You have your mistress near to you
Whom on you lavish love
While silent I must still remain
As you two walk above
My children cry out unto me
The shame and pain is great
Madame Monsieur in a marriage such
Would you not separate?

My marriage it was prearranged

In it I had no say

But passed was I like a prize

Which with the losers pay

Our parents say that we would stand

Content to e'er be used

No thought gave they that one of us

Might find another love instead

They joined us fast forevermore

And said happy I should be

That my mates parents did consent

For their child to marry me

No more I said of their choice

I'd try to make them proud

I'd live as they believed I should

Go along with the new crowd

For years I've silently this withstood

As my mate a lover knew

Ah Madame Monsieur as I watched this

Would you've stood and watched it too?

Alas now I can no more stay

Go on the way I've been

I seek divorce from my bonds

Too much split love I've seen

My mate insist that I must stay

Tho my mate a lover keeps

And swears to ever keep that love

Ever held there above me

That lover I must learn to love

Respect and hold in awe

And silently hold deep inside

Hurtful memories I recall

I must not recall to my mate

The way I've been disgraced

The way I must bow in humility

To one who has me displaced

I plead, I beg, I pray, I cry

I curse, protest and plan

Madame Monsieur thru all my pains

Do you still not understand?

My house or home is Canada

My name La Belle Province Quebec

My mate the English Countryman

Who mostly show me disrespect

My parents Confederation were

Wherefrom this mate I gained

My children are the Francophone

As the English call my name

The lover that my house upset

The one whom my home laid waste

The one to whom I fail to bow

Is the monarchic English race

I find no reason why I should

Bend down in shame my head

And live as second-class citizen

While they rule o'er high instead

I love my home my Canada

But thru them I feel deep pain

Madame Monsieur if you understand

Tell me why should I remain?

If we are still a colony

How can we a Nation status hold

If not then why in 100 years

Haven't we brought our Constitution home

Why were we forcefully sent out

To fight on England's stand

Why pay we highest tribute of all

To a Queen of a foreign land

Why is it that those we elect

Before they can do our wishes

Must swear allegiance to a crown

Which represents the British

Why must even our Prime Minister
Be but a servant one who gives
A pass upwards for final consent
Our laws to her representatives
Had France instead the war did win
And we stood opposite our stand
Madame Monsieur in this free free world
Could you pay allegiance to a foreign land?

No foreign land it be you say
Tho it lies far across the seas
It is your fathers motherland
Where then does that leave me
My parents motherland was France
Where in cultured pride we grew
They gave it up to build this home
Anglophone then why cant you
We seek not to hold fast unto
The past ways of our fathers lives
We hoped instead to intermix
Our cultures, dreams and strives
Long past weaned, we in adulthood
Now want our fates to choose
To be proud of our home Canada
Each others rights un-abused

We do not ask you to become
Full French or live as we do
Yet Madame Monsieur you seem to think
We should full English be for you.

We want what you have long enjoyed
The right to feel proud and free
But under Britain's sovereignty
The defeated still feel we
We want the right to stand and sing
Oh Canada thru our land
And pay allegiance to our Flag
Proud to be a Canadian
We want the right to chose to give
Our lives when Canada calls
'Gainst any foe from anywhere
But obligated to none at all
We want to hold in proud respect
Our country's name World wide
To stand alone unique and tall
No apron-strings to us tied
We want to go where e'er we feel
Across our wide wide land
And be Madame Monsieur a Canadian
Not a French nor Englishman.

We want our children to look up
Not at our past and what has been
But at their own full futures free
As one people one Canadian
Our cultures past mixed with yours
Can only give glory to our land
The day and hour and minute when
We can all swear allegiance Canadian
No more to crowns and heirs to come
No more to Kings or Queens
But to our Maple Leaf forever
This alone it is our dreams
To elect our leaders one and all
From among our fellowmen
And have them swear to serve us all
Be we Canadians or Canadiens
We can no longer quietly sit
While these our cultures segregate
Madame Monsieur help us change this
Else we be forced to separate.

For all these years we've silent sat
And watched our union fall
As you held unto England's hand
Like a loved mistress thru it all

Despised like an unwanted spouse

Am I expected yet to wait

And watch my children call her Mom

While she determines still their fate

I've spoken, begged and pleaded out

Try to make you understand

That our home she threatens being here

Yet you cling to your woman

No more in shame can I live

In a home I helped to build

But rather I'll another start

Wherein I can proudly live

I'd love to keep our home intact

Where you and I can equal live

Madame Monsieur tell her leave our home

While we've yet a chance to build.

Now you and I can look up to

Our Country whole and grand

Turn our energies to developments

For and with our countryman

Undivided then in stand and goal

Our wills and wants the same

Our pledge of faithful servitude

To within our home remain

Then far across this World of ours
The nations all shall say
That cultures united can work out
We the proof they all will say
No more an English nor a French
A foreigner to be
But a full unique Canadian
From sea thru land to sea
I've said my piece Madame Monsieur
In hope you will realize
I love my home my Canada
Let's not let England it divide.
For we have built this home of ours
The true North strong and free
Lets leave our pasts far far behind
Make full Canadians of you and me...

A ship a world unto itself,
each crew member
but a drifting island

He Walks The Noisy Corridors

He walks the noisy corridors of his prison

With iron walls, iron roof and floor

Pacing ever looking at the gauges

Which tells him his ship is safe secure

His temperature tester is his right hand

His nose fire detector is unsurpassed

His quick eye the ever present monitor

His trained ear, tho deaf, hears him the heart

He walks the iron corridors of his prison

Wherein beats the heart of every ship

Where work to keep the purring engines going

Goes on as he sustains their lives each trip

A quick glance and a little drop of oil here

Here now a touch with blade of screwdriver slim

A nut to tighten or a valve to loosen

Each done unseen by anyone by him

The gauges each a thousand times he sees them

Yet a flutter change of pointer he'll detect

Like computer then his brain in these will enter

Make sure they're 'right 'til he'll pass again 'n' check

A twist, a turn, a little more is given

Or then again perhaps taken away

The revs he's so constantly controlling

Like food to sustain the engines life each day

He walks the noisy corridors of his prison

In haggard looking oil-soaked coveralls

With minute holes or paste-on cover patches

Where heat or tear or acid on did fall

He's like a king in his royal kingdom

He's like a pauper crawling in the mud

He's like an artist touching up the paintwork

He's like a prisoner here but he's in love

'Tis love that keeps this being ever moving

Slow slowly like a treadmill walker goes

'Round an engine room in thought filled silence

While loud around him the engines whine 'n' roar

The Engineer -- the true engine worker

The one whom on the ships for life rely

That dirty seldom seen participator

Without whom all ships engines would die

A doctor and a husband of the innards
Each diagnostic word must be correct
Each self-assured decision is so critical
Yet done so oft often without respect
The lights that glitter and the drinking water
The toilets, galley, elevators and the fans
The lifeboats and the doors that easy open
The steering gear and wheelhouse he commands

The air and oil in tubes for operation
The rudder which guides the ship along
The prop which underwater the ship powers
Each he must know and ever check upon
He walks the noisy corridors of his prison
In day or night all hours without rest
Tho seldom seen he keeps the ship a-running
Content that in his job he does his best

Yes, he walks the noisy corridors of his prison
With iron walls, iron roof and floor
Pacing ever -- looking at the gauges
Which tells him that his ship is safe, secure

Untimely But Timely Justice

And it happened that in a land there was a young virginal woman who having been abducted from her father's home was savagely beaten and raped. Now when her abductor rapist was brought before the high court of the land behold the Supreme Monarch judge sitting there looked at the perpetrator of these wrongs and said, "Behold I find you guilty by your own admission and hereby do sentence you to pay five cents for these wrongs -- now come on let's go to dinner."

And the victim became pregnant thereafter by a kind and gentle man and bore him a son. Now while seeking daily bread for his wife and son, this man was set upon robbed, beaten and shortly did die from his wounds. And once again the culprit who did cause his death came before the Supreme Monarch judge and admitted his guilt. And the judge smiled and placing an arm around the culprit's shoulders said unto him, "Now you know you shouldn't do things like this, pay the clerk the five cents fine and try control yourself."

As time went on, the son of the raped woman grew to manhood and behold the son of the rapist also grew to manhood and thru their adolescent years the son of the rapist teased and ridiculed the son of the raped for being a son of a woman who had been raped by his father and whose father had been killed by his father. And the raped woman said unto her son, "Behold where ignorance abounds be thee silent and patient less in a fit of righteous anger you exact the punishment upon the ignorant for the sons of the father." And the son paid heed to her words and smote not the son of the rapist, but rather did try to ignore or humor him as he continued in his ways.

Then behold one day as the son of the raped was accosted by the son of the rapist. The son of the raped looked full into the eyes of the son of the rapist and said "You gotta walk life's lonely valley, you're gonna walk once by yourself, you won't know when justice will enter, but you're gonna pay like everyone else." And the son of the rapist walked away laughing and lived for but seven more years in which time his worldly good and estates were destroyed by fire, his father as an alcoholic died alone in the street and a cancer raked the insides of his being for five years without relief. And lying on his deathbed in extreme pain, the face of the son of the raped appeared unto him and a voice said unto him, "Behold thy hour is at hand and the sins of thy father are visited down upon you to the fullest measure of their injustice wroth upon others." And he died leaving naught upon the face of the earth to carry on his name and with him, ended an era of degradation.

So too one time a race of peoples were abducted, beaten, raped, enslaved and murdered and after hundreds of years their perpetrators were freed of their crime and soothed their conscience by the payment of five cents for each of their then held slaves. From these abducted peoples come I seeking to live in peace, fellowship and in equality but behold if this then be not possible stand warned of the righteousness of my wrath upon the day and persons when it I vent. Let not thy ignorance cause my anger forth to boil for deep and long contained lie the hurts and anguish of my many raped and murdered peoples who cry out yet for justice from the enfolds of their shallow graves...

> Better to have been
> a beaten Slave and lived
> than a Master and alive
> in deathlike shame forever

There Is A Cancer In This Land

There is a cancer in this land
Which touches every heart
It is hate towards our fellowman
But why why did it start
We know not how or who it caused
Save what's in Holy Writ
But we have lived and seen it work
And felt the brunt of it
We've seen our lands all overgrown
With virgin majesty green
Burnt and hewn down to let in
A destructive corruptive scheme
We've felt the mother Earth give pull
As from it we were torn
As slaves in chains to live and die
Even unto our kids unborne
Hate is the Cancer which we see
Slow spread until it stands
A big and sick and whitely mass
Which kills every black man
An open running sickening sore
Which from it maggots breathe
To try to eat away our wills

To stifle increase of our seed

Within us too there lies alas

A cancer of hate like in you

Which has been growing from the start

In return for the wrongs you did do

This cancer is the hardest now

Of the diseases which we face

We can only conquer it with love

And recognition of the Human race

Oh why cant we now both reject

The ways of our peoples past

And learn to live in harmony

and a freedom which can last

This cancer of hate burns deep inside

Of you and me alike

Let's strive to live above our pride

Let's forget who's black or white

Men often marry for the security
of the thighs that bind
while a lot of women marry looking
for a leaning post

Little Girl In Quiet Sleep

Little girl in quiet sleep

Little boy in joyous play

Little dog in yard doth stay

Why oh why why run away

Little girl you've grown so fast

Leaving dolls loved in the past

Leaving ropes and swings and things

Seeking now those glittering rings

Little boy you're behind prison bars

Your future by law now marred

As you try to understand your wrong

Your mind goes back to times gone on

Little dog now lying dead

A bullet swift entered your head

And chained you could not even run

You only barked and that in fun

Alas, alas there but remains

The truth that caused you three such pain

You did not see and did not know

Your lives were doomed in that ghetto

Little girl when you'd been raped

The judge free let that white escape

Claiming that you led him on

Now to prostitution you have gone

Little boy you but spoke once too often

Of wrongs which put your friends in prison

So you too they did incarcerate

An endless prison terms your fate

Oh little dog you could've barked free

If your owner wasn't black like me

And no one ever would have sought

To end your life with a pistol shot

You three have lived and learned so fast

The pain and hurt of years gone past

You did no wrongs all you did lack

You were not white you three were blacks

I've Been Reading Past Histories

I've been reading past histories written

Of peoples and places and men

Of how the new world was discovered

By whom with what and when

Of tales which around them was gathered

By women and men of olden time

Of voyages and of those they conquered

Of past ancestors of yours and of mine

In books you've written I've pondered

The beauty your cultures have reached

I've marveled at your majestical wonder

And listened to words that you've preached

Your ways of life your wants and your Jesus

Your ideas of right and of wrong

I've taken and made mine examples

I've praised your blood heroes in song

I've been the feel of your sorrows

Suffering in your stead the pain

For you I've been willing to steal or borrow

Ne'er conscious of disgracing my name

From distant far shores of my homeland

I've come to you bounded in chains

To render to you in your new land

Works unequalled, unpaid for unclaimed

Down stooping I've bent and been humbled

Contented the last place to take

If my humility would serve but to heighten

To strengthen esteem your estate

Now alas I have given my past life

My fathers and mothers to you

My children have bent to your pleasure

Yet received we ne'er gratitude due

Our hard years of toiling in silence

Has built up our minds bodies strong

While we waited and waited in pretence

Now at last here we shall right the wrong

No longer shall you live in freedom

Not giving to us rights we crave

We're willing ready to die for our freedom

No longer shall we be your slave

A rut and a grave differs only in their diggers,

a rut you dig, a grave is dug for you

When I Was But A Tiny Babe

When I was but a tiny babe
You took and taught me well
All the things which you believed
Would keep me out of hell
You gave me values you possessed
Which you had once found true
But somehow you can't realize
The pain you put me through
You who had learned to hate yourself
Because of your dreary past
You who wished to unkink your hair
And to whiten your black ass
You who in disgust would gaze
At one darker yet than you
You who brainwashed me to believe
This shit as still you do
You made a life of misery
You brought me pain and shame
You whitewashed my brain until
My skin became to me a shame
You raised me thru my childhood
As best in ignorance you could

Recalling to me a thousand times

The goals for which you stood

Alas, alas you poor dumb man

You took my guts and pride

You ruined what there was in me

You tried to whiten me inside

You tried you tried O God you tried

'Til I did to you bow

'Til I lost my true self somewhere

God look at your creation now

Look at the one you made to stand

Shamed of past and skin so black

Look at the shell you did brainwash

Till a quiet subservient you got back

Then look afar, afar away,

And here's what you will see

I lived I grew I tried to be a man

You killed the Man in me

Beware: Fish not where you swim less thee
increase to thyself the endangerment of sharks.

Help Me Help Me Help Me

Help me Help me Help me
I've called and called in vain
For 300 years in dark despair
In want and grief and pain
I've learnt your awkward language
I obey your laws so strange
I laugh and sing and listen to
Your merriment so strange
I drive upon your highways
I walk along your streets
I dress in clothes you did design
I've shoes made by you on my feet
I work your menial labour
I eat your poisoned foods
I breathe the air you contaminate
I study in your schools
I apply my thoughts to standards
Which conform with what you've set
I even worship now your God
But I haven't pleased you yet
I have two eyes two arms two legs
One body just like yours

I eat I sleep I hurt I feel

So why can't I open yet the doors

I wish to you no evil

I care not for your treasures

I try to avoid all hurt and strife

And to bring all joy and pleasure

Yet after taking full stock I find

That my existence you still condemn

Why try to take away from me

Life's sustenance my friend

I've done my all in every way

'Til there's but one thing I lack

I don't want or envy your white skin

Why do you hate me cause mine's BLACK

Express yourself
dream a wild dream,
reach for the unreachable
and may it all today
be yours for the taking

To Serve My People One And All

To serve my people one and all

To save all that come from a fall

To work that they freedom may know

To spread joy wheresoever I go

To give of myself 'til the last

To right all the wrongs of the past

To strive to return to my lands

All things taken by the foreign grands

To be willing to live or to kill

With the hope of one day setting free

All the people I know who have known slavery

To be willing to die -- for to give my life in exchange

For this great Quest is my only true aim

For I know that the blood -- sweat -- and tears

Of my peoples for hundreds of years

Shall not go un-revenged thru my dear Saviour's ears

And my soul shall find only its rest

When these wrongs have been righted -- but best

Then my aim in life will be fulfilled

When my people can come and go as they will

And their world will be bettered by this

Tho one man or a nation apart

Do strive thru its life and its death

To show that all men should be FREE

And all will then know sure and well

That we've strove thru life's bitter Hell

To prove -- to show -- and to attain

What was ours by right -- Yet denied by their might

'Till at last they have tasted and know

That for that freedom -- a man -- to the grave will go

And we shall rest assured -- and blessed -- and free

When all among men we too like MEN can enjoy LIBERTY

Tho slow swings the pendulum of life its balance is perfect and thus will in time reach the other side.

Tongue Can't Tell

Tongue can't tell

Nor Actions show

The Love I have

For you and so

- - I THINK - -

I'll chisel it in Zinc

I like the sacrificial zinc

gives its life to protect

those nearest to it.

Listen To Me You Bigots All

Listen to me you bigots all

Its been over three hundred years

I've lived slaved suffered died and all

To give restrain to your goddamn fears

Fears -- Yes you uptight bastards

Too lazy to work your goddamn fields

Too lazy to prepare your goddamn meals

Too lazy to construct your goddamn wheels

Too lazy and afraid to even screw like me

You loathsome fear-filled son of a bitch

Who from my father's blood got rich

Who took my nations golden ores

Who made my sisters into whores

Then after you had us all enslaved

And sent millions to an early grave

Now you pretend ignorance of it

You bigoted bastard hush your shit

You raped my islands large and small

And peopled them in bygone days

You master of the seas and all

You led the trade in the slaving days

You knighted the prick who did start

From Africa my peoples to remove

You grew richer for the bloody part
This your own written history do prove
You took away my hopes and rights
My relatives you did segregate
And now still you mother whites
Still try my young to separate
Oh stop your shit and leave your throne
Your days of worldly power is dead
And if my goddamn peoples aren't left alone
I swear to burn out your asses red

Criminals are not born, they are the by-products
of constant police officer harassments

You Are Perfect

You are perfect, perfect it seems to me
No one else could more perfect be
I guess that this the reason we are through
I couldn't be quite as perfect as you
I hoped that someday there might be
Some of your perfectness in me
But since it's not my destiny
I'll be content to leave you perfectly

One could term sexually maladjusted women

as being constant virgins

and sexually maladjusted men as deadheads

So Many Thousand Miles Away

So many thousand miles away

You live upon your Bigots throne

You sleep in velvet cloth all day

Yet still won't leave us blacks alone

Give us our Goddamn islands back

That's all that we do demand

Leave our homelands to our peoples black

We can rule right our own island

We have no need of you

Or of your goddamn pain and shit

That we for centuries have gone thru

With your Imperial seal on it

So call your ass lickers back

Away from our sound and sight

We'd rather live in a shanty shack

Than as a slave of you goddamn whites

Your great whore you do venerate

Is but an extension of the past

Who lived and prospered by the fate

As she profited from each blacks ass

Black man and women girls and boys

Like cattle in slave stalls did lie

Where they were beaten used killed enjoyed

On auction day some there did die

You sold the mother to one bastard

While the child to another bigot went

You shafted the entire black race faster

Than any pestilence heaven has sent

You killed those who did try to show

That your slaving ways were wrong

Then you cold-blooded hypocrites did go

To your white church to sing your goddamn song

Well past time is over and the time

Has changed and now this is our land

Move out your ass while there's still time

Recall your bigot expatriate whites Oh England

Wishing you the very best on this your special day

May you fulfill your fantasies and realize your dreams

...Oka

A shot ran out...

And then a shout...

I thought I saw a move...

'Twas but a native Indian...

Trying to escape obscure...

A soldier aims his gun again

A woman and child lies

Upon a grassy golfing tee

There by her man she dies

What reason for I inwards ask

This carnage and this rage

Which tends to but backwards turn

The nations civilizing page

For surely one can plainly see

The rule of law outcast

As for political revengefulness

This crisis has come to pass

One angry vengeful leader yet

Burns inside for what he lost

Sees here a chance to even out

His hurt pride at Native's cost

So now he will at last exact

From those innocent that be

His failed plan of own nationhood

Their lives he'll make unfree

A country's leader giving leave

To a statesman gone quite mad

To use a country's armament

To revenge a deal gone bad

A country's peoples standing by

While its helpless are laid tow

Will live to reap it just rewards

Watch itself so likewise go

And from the blood and pride cast down

Will rise new pride to fight again

When native man woman and child

Will return their rights to claim

Twill be no more just an Indian

But an Indian's nation stand

To revenge this final white outrage

Taking back their blood soaked land.

270990 DC

Law enforcement truly
describes many policemen;
Law and Force Men

> Seaweed -- the original flotsam
> subtly recapturing the unspent resources
> of nature for conservational release
> Unto another generation.

Peace At Last Then Shall Know I

If my sense of love must dim
If my sense of passion die
Why should I remain and suffer
With my heart, my ears, my eye
Why must sounds return the memories
Of the ways life used to be
While the sights show ancient pictures
Lived now as once lived by me
What the heart craves for so useless
When the holders cares have gone
And the mind knows it is hopeless
Yet this empty life goes on.

Let my sense of love diminish
Let my sense of passion cease
Let my life flow out like raindrops
'Long some hot and dusty street

Pull away my heart from caring
And from my ears remove the sounds
Blind my eyes to renewed pictures
Which for me no more comes 'round
Let my mind fall empty useless
Let my brain no deep thoughts hold
And my body return to the ashes
Wherefrom it once was formed.

Then alas I shall know peace
Seek no passion more to find
See and hear and think no love notes
Want no lover warmly mine
And my body it shall wither
Blow away or simply die
Then my heart will beat no longer
Peace at last then shall know I...

Being No One is above the law
except for our police
we should rename them as our "NO ONES"

The Sands Of Time

The beach scene brings back memories

Of long ago and far away

Of other beach scenes in the mind

Where free I frolicked played

Where life had not yet turned the glass

Of time to bottom run

And time itself seemed evermore

Destined to onwards run

The fleeting sands of time at last

Must onwards run to ruin

And cause each player caught therein

To pay the price be the undoing

And so when I had placed the hope

Of life on one last plateau

The stealing hands of time they moved

To do that which best they do

The sands of time these hands did turn

By placing the fragile hourglass

Upon the hill where it could not

Be reached as time it slowly passed

Yet in the crevice of its arms

It held the sands of time

To tease me and torment me yet

While life's peace I tried to find

Oh cruel time keeper of the fates

You who knows the hearts of men

Return upright the cursed hourglass

That I in life may live and love again

Let not the sands of fleeting time

So uselessly run out

When so much waits for me to do

When my life has so much doubt

Oh sands of fleeting time recall

The loves and life that yet could be

If but thy fragile hourglass

Did not hold as hostage me

The fleeting hands of time hold you

Oh sands of time shake free

And with your new found freedom then

Reach out and too free me...

18/7/87

May the bounteousness of your thoughts be
the only limits of today's realities for you

"The Liberate Man"

Be a man my son I said

Let no woman pull you down

Stand tall and straight on principle

Such as you've set around

Holdfast to rights of living

Keep strong your freedoms fight

Be a man my son I beg you

Caring not who says you're right

===========

"How can I this accomplish

If I in this world must grow

Have I not to fall in love and be

Cared and needed for fore I go

Shall I not find toil to keep me

Build a house with hope and pride

Seek someone to share it with me

And by the norms of old abide?

How can I this accomplish

If I follow not life's plan

Have you secrets learnt to give me
Which'll more free me make as man?
Have you lessons learnt while living
Which may cause to ease my pain
Which may help me to walk equal free
With women and with men?

Have you learnt from life the reason
Why as man we negative be
Why our lives in guilt and fear abound
Seemingly passed on endlessly?
Have you answers why we so react
To every whim, sigh, word or look
Like we're guilty for each woman's tears
Which flows free as from a brook?

Give to me a voice for feelings
To my heart outlets for pains
Rest my soul from guilt and turmoil
Ease my mind from fear and shame
Wet my eyes when hurt o'erpowers
Release my angers when it's due
Let me laugh and see emotions free
Given these I'll be a man for you"

==========

Be a man my son I beg you

This is but your right in life

To stifle not your feelings

To release your held uptights

To laugh loud out and freely

To cry, giggle, smirk or clown

To be all that you feel to be

To let no sarcasm pull you down

To be as proud of tear-filled eyes

As you are of love filled heart

To feel free to fail and ask for help

Or to for years make not a start

To be a selfish seeming one

'Til your terms are fully met

To give of yourself in measure full

Equal only to what you get

To love a woman or a man

In ways equal and free

To hide not affections that you feel

Just 'cause someone else may see

To stay or go yet procreate

To accept or reject your young

To have one woman thru-out life

Or have none tie you down

To flutter like a sparrow

From tree to nest or ground

To give your all just to yourself

Or all of you ever spread around

To build a home or mansion

Or just a playboy's den

Or live in tent or sleeping bag

Your roadmap as your friend

To be a loner till you feel

The need for a one-night stand

Then ease your need and move along

This is your right as man

To ask but once and beg not

For naught in life you choose

To remember always there remains

Some other who won't refuse

To make of light the many wiles

Used to try to tie you down

To cling long to your freedom

To be free to move around

To live a life as fully

While you still single lie

To be afraid not of tomorrow

As your first decades pass you by

To not live by the age old story

That manhood means wife and home

That a man who's over thirty

Should long have ceased to roam

To feel free to trust your feelings

To laugh at decisions wrong

To let past trials pass you by

Keep in your heart a song

To walk with arms around a man

In friendship clear and free

To offer woman companionship

Or pass and just let them be

To greet no one in anger

Fight for no woman's name

Feel free to laugh at ridicule

Unashamed to turn in fear

To see each man as equal

So to hold woman's virtue too

Not up nor down but on a par

With that offered her by you

To spread these things of manhood

'Til man is liberate and free

No longer guilt to ever feel

Nor to woman bend a knee

'Til on an even landing

You and she can lie and say

I want you come on over

Or I don't need you go away

'Til she can speak her mind still

And give you too that right

To voice your needs, wants and fears

Without getting uptight

To play and joke and frolic

Or just to passive lay

To take just your satisfaction

Get up and walk away

To not be held responsible

For what she makes of life

To keep her as a bedmate, friend

Lover, mistress or as wife

To lose that Godlike feature

Which they would have us keep

That binds us to works grindstone

By hour, by day, by week

To be a man who's able

To do all that a woman can

Save bear the child you give her

The one thing needed from a man

To realize that a woman's strength

Out-lasts what to man is given

For in their wily ways secured

They've enjoyed what for we've striven
And still they hold to bargain yet
What they feel alone they own
Unthinking of the vast reserves
Out waiting -- somewhere -- alone
So be a man my son I beg you
Cast not your years away
Fall not behind the norms that be
Do not their old games play
Stand first my son for happiness
But make it first your own
Give not one thing in bargaining
'Less you first satisfy your own
These words and lessons given you
Are of years spent and wisdom learnt
So follow each one carefully
And a man free I will have grown
The things you ask be given you
You'll find you've had from birth
So be a man happy free my son
Then my life'll have had some worth

Feminists can never be known as Mastered-pieces

These Are My Hands

These are my hands, these are my arms

these are my fingers

This is my head here is my heart my soul divine

These are my legs these are my feet on which I stand

To tell the world with these my words that you are mine

This is my child this is my wife this is my country

This is the Ideal firm in my mind for which I live

I have but one heart and one life to give now

But I'll remain proud only if myself I give

I'll walk along the streets oh so narrow

I'll walk along besides the whispering waterfalls

I live and love my everyday and I enjoy life

And I enjoy it all -- being myself

I do not crave to be some other person

I do not care to rise up to worldly fame

As long as I can be myself and hold my head high

As long as I am myself with a clean and spotless name

As long as the rivers flow and the rains fall

As long as seasons come and seasons go

I'll live my life or give my life to you love

As long as with you I can watch myself truly grow

Earth, Heaven and you
Truly the most glorious
of all the creations imaginable

I Walked Upon Your Street

I walked upon your street alone

You called to me in friendship

You gave me shelter from the cold

And food to take on my trip

I stood outside your door at night

In thirst and want and pain

You gave me water cool and sweet

You put ointments on my veins

I crawled among the ghettos' streets

I ate garbage from the gutters

You took me -- placed me in your bed

With no thoughts like the others

I've tried and tested you and found

Your love so true and steadfast

I know you are a friend to men

There's no sufferer that you would pass

And thus it is that I now take

This crown and place upon thee

The blessings of the God of Love

Your reward throughout eternity

For I am he that hunger shook

And thirst and pain had weakened

The ghetto lad you warmly took

And had his needs all straightened

To man you have so oft appeared

A fool to waste your time

But they're the fools who knew me not

As I appeared as the least, to mine

We Must Seek Fields

We must seek fields

In which wild seeds to sow

In which in youth to allow

Our wild oats to grow

How else could we

Expect to let down roots

To support a stable

Tree of adult life

Nov 9 1973

Human Wolves

Because I am not one of their kind and pack

I am bruised, I am wounded, I am beaten

My cries for help they go unheard

My pleas for succour go unheeded

Yet still I try, I try to hold on

Yet still I cling to my sanity...

The pack of wolves surround me

On all sides close they in for my blood

Snarling and biting I see their fangs flash

And know that they wait in their cowardness

Know that they hesitate only because of the light...

For these creatures of the darkness

Work their savagery under the cover of sightlessness

And devour their prey when they can least be seen

For this is their cowardly nature...

And I, tho laying broken, bruised, bleeding and alone

Without a hand to help or move me to assist

Seek solace in my single small and trusty blade

And in my three remaining unspent shots

to which I cling

Alas 'tis evening and around my body close they gather

These wolves which soon shall of me a meal make

Which shall my last blood drink away
As warm yet my flesh
they in their savagery consummate...
Then knowing this am I not in my right
To raise my gun and try at least survival
To use my last life's gasp with single blade
To take away -- one -- two -- a few with me
That dying tho I shall -- yet with my life's end
A small recompense for injustice suffered
I shall at last exact.

090993-1

Sunlight

Sunlight
-- Clear air --
Clean waters
Cloudy skies
-- Foggy banks --
Murky depths
Each but a reflection
of its opposite
Each but a glance
at the other side...

Pity The Man

Pity the man who waits on a virgin

Who waits on a man who waits on a virgin

When they both are virgins no more

Gone is the high hopes he highly had hoped for

For hopes he had hoped for too high he finds gone

Lost are the passionate promises

She had him long with lured

With passion subdued

Her long promises to him are now lost

Life is a matter of fact now betwix them

Betwix them a fact now life has no matter at all

Now pity the man lonely

Who must seek the extra non-virgin

Who seeks the man lonely

Who seeks the extra non-virgin

To hold in her arms when his life now is cold

For cold lies the life which is built on false promises

For false promises are empty

And the life built is fast o'er

Take heed then you young men who seek for the virgin

Who seek for the young men who seek for the virgin

For lonely the long life which is paid for that treasure

That lone one time in life

Long which repays you in pleasure

Then pity the man dumb who waits on the virgin

Who waits on the man dumb who waits on the virgin

When both they are virgins no more

The title MS should only be applied
to divorced women for marriage severed

The Love Boat

Love boat break thy route
Leave thy southern waters warm
To sail the inside passage
'Cross where Haida Indians
The Nootka and the Tsimpsean
Once all in longboats brave
Did cross o'er on the tide.

And yet thy beauty beams
Out like your painted portrait
Or like the glass clear video scene
One of you often sees
Alive and real you pass us by
Alive no -- more a fantasy
No more a dream of celluloid
Your wake forms on the tide.

What grace you lines are showing
What form you hull entails
What beauty and what majesty
You impart as by you sail
The glimmer of sun's golden sheen
Turns evening waters gold
With your imprint of blue and white
You sit a vision to behold

The islands small drift you by
The seagulls soar and fall
The late summer's moon in half
Waits to paint you full soft gold
What more could then on ask for
As your form we gaze upon
Except the chance we too
May one day sail you on

Move on then as clouds linger
Faint on yonder far horizon
To cause a frame your picture
To encase and warm envelope
Love boat Pacific Princess
So named and brought to fame
A hope for those who seek it
A refuge for those in shame

A place of life and laughter
A Shangri-La on the seas
An unending dream to seek after
A belief for all you be
Sail on sail on love boat sail on
'Til you journeys full are o'er
Then in the peace and deserved rest
Rest you in love in Heaven's bower.

Rating A Lady Lover...

A lady friend once asked me

As we lay upon the bed

To rate her on a score of one to ten

As I looked at her in wonder

She said she'd like to know

If I thought her good enough to love again

She went on then to tell how

Thru the many men she's had

This need to know seems her to e'er possess

For tho she often makes love

Each time she always asks

Her lover to rate her sex progress

And what would I tell my male friends

If ever they should ask

About our times shared in a rendezvous

Would I tell them she was good in bed

Or how best would I describe

The ways she loved and what best did she do

Would I remember her in future

And look her up again

Or was her impression on me but faint

Did she arouse the animal passion

Deep within my soul

Or just the lovemaking male's instinct

Would I be glad I laid with her

Or would I recall the times

And say she was nothing to shout about

Or would I get a feeling warm

As our moments I recalled

And would a hot smile play about my mouth

And tomorrow as I awakened

Would I again be turned on

As I lay there and watched her slowly dress

And if I could back remember

Would I tell her of the girl

Whom I lay with that had me most deep impressed...

I gave thought to her questions

But did not to them reply

As thru my thoughts memories fast raced

As I recalled so many whom

I'd laid with warm and hot

Their forms their figures and the passion on their face

Then in reply I asked her

How she I now should grade

As but three ways I'd lain with women thru the years

I'd made love to some had sex with others hot and hard

And lastly quite a few I'd screwed as well

I went on as she watched me

To explain in full detail

That a man by these a woman he does rate

For to all tho they be a great piece of tail

It depends in which category she's been great

For those that a man lay with

With love deep in his heart

Are always held the best of those he's had

No matter if their actions

Or their aftermaths should fail

He would never rate their moments shared as bad

Those whom 'twas only sex with

And the others seem to fall

In but two other reaches of his mind

The ones who shared only

For to fill their hungried need

Or those that hoped some reward from him to find

So love I will not rate you

For to do so would me shame

As you may have changed my feelings

Deep and true

Just take the love I offer

Love like I've taken what you gave

And rest assured then I'll never forget you.

Fortunate the Prince of today --

he needs not a frog's hideous disguise

when a simple cloak of poverty will easily suffice.

<u>Oh Maker</u>

Oh Maker,

In my idle plenty

I knew not Happiness

therefore I pray:

May my wealth sustain me

when my health is gone

but until then

may I be blessed

with no shortages

of the menial toil

wherein lies

the true joy of Life.

Strange the married person

who thinks not of a lover,

Lucky the married person who can

A Grim Recollection...

I recall a tiny inland

In the blue Caribbean Sea

One of three ruled o'er by Britain

Thru days of darkest slavery

On that inland stands a castle

Built of stone by Black man's hands

With walls thick and open dungeon

On that Island home Cayman

There it was in that same castle

That a woman Black and brave

Gave she birth to one last man-child

Tho she yet remained a Slave

Nursed she yet her tiny infant

Helping him to manhood grow

On the hope of promised Emancipation

Would allow him freedom to know

As this man-child she gave birth to

Grew within the castle's walls

News came down of freedoms message

For the Black man one and all

She in shock in awe and in wonder

Slowly came to the meaning clear

No more bound to be forever

Slaves now are freed everywhere

And this woman old and weak now

Could not take the strain in heart

Bidst she farewell to the others

Told her son they now must part

Told him of her life before him

Of the ways the slaves had lived

Of his past ancestors brought here

Of the many proud now killed

Let him understand true fully

That the white man had not changed

That this freedom he now gave them

'Twas only for a long fight exchanged

Showed she him that now survival

Meant the man would cunning be

Keeping down thru hate and pressures

Those who sought to full free be

Then she said tho small this measure

Grasp it son and build a dream

One whereon you 'gain will never

See the pains like past I've seen

Build a home a hope a future

Build upon the pride you own

Give your young the truth of Africa

Help them love it as their own

Give them cause to stand forever

With their eyes 'gainst any man

Proud and free and never bending

No more again to fear any man

Let them know who built this Island

Let our history past stand strong

Let them e'er be proud of their blackness

Let them not forget the white man's wrong

Let my son this be your mission

A request as here I lie

Then within my grave so peaceful

Content I'll stay when I die

Taking firm his hand she held It

To her heart which fluttered low

And with a look of peaceful pleasure

On her face -- Granddad watched her go...

The difference between alimony and prostitution

depends on which one is left satisfied

You Can't Teach Me to Be Black

You may have taught me many things
But you can't teach me what I lack
For I was born even as I am
You can't teach me to be black

You taught me to be first ashamed
You filled my insides with fright
You tried your best to teach me
I should respect you 'cause you're white

My life belongs to you you feel
Nothing must I answer back
But thru It all you still have failed
You can't teach me to be black

You showed me well how in ways
You could keep my life in pain
Each pinnacle I strove to reach
You'd cast me off again

'Til inadequate you'd have me feel
Like one who the senses lack
For all my years you've tried and tried
To teach me to be black

You tell me that my anger now
Which is in me deeply stored
Is really but my problem which

I should quietly try to cure

You said too sensitive am I

In remembering life's past track

Instead of letting past be past

And learning to be black

You say to turn my cheek again

As so oft in the past I've done

And forevermore take compromise

For the wrongs I have not done

You say to overlook and smile

To my past happy ways go back

And forget the man that lives in me

Once more learn how to be black

In ways so subtle you me ask

A slave to yet remain

A lackey and a servant who's

Contented in my shame

Try not to rise too high you say

My place I should know is back

To follow e'er behind your lead

To you this is being black

As long as I bow down my head

Long as I deny me self-respect

Long as I'm willing with you to agree

You need not to keep me checked

As long as I let all you wish

My deeds become in fact

You'll feel secured and satisfied

That I am being black

To you a black is someone who

You tolerate when around

A thing which should you look upon

It's like dirt upon clean ground

A being which should grateful be

That you have let It live

This lesson long you have taught

But it to me you cannot give

For I have lived too long within

This skin which I still wear

I've learnt the truth of ages past

And why you live in fear

I've seen the angers you did heap

Upon my ancestor's backs

And thru it all unknown to you

I've known how to be black

I've known that freedom is for all

Who stands and for it fights

I've found that speaking out but helps

To regain our hidden rights

I've seen you bend and cower low

When full I straight my back

You live in fear whene'er you see

Me live truly as a black

And so now again you say to me

Prehaps I'm the one to blame

The cause for hatred that I feel

May be but self-inflicted shame

You try to reason others out

Make it seem true fault they lack

While saying maybe I see too much

In just my being black

You who have never and cannot

Ever live my skin within

Still feign that you can understand

My angers hurts and pains

You who so shallow seek to find

Me at fault in spite of facts

Are but another reason why

I now must live full black

If you and yours had let us be

To live long our lives as men

No worry would you have known

When you saw us now and then

But no instead you high did feel

Determined we to keep held back

Ne'er forgetting past pains we knew

When you enslaved fully we blacks

So rest your lip and save your breath

No more in silence will I sit

As you walk o'er me every day

Expecting me e'er to tolerate it

To never speak on move or fight

'Gainst your old ways brought back

But this time alas we stand proud

That's what it means to be true black

To live as human beings all

To flight or kill or die

If only to show to the world

You're no better man than I

To tell the truth that all should know

How we better are in fact

For 'twas you who stole our peoples all

And made slaves of we blacks

Yes you may have taught me many things

But you can teach me ne'er that fact

To be a man full proud and free

Means first I must be Black...

Forgive Me For Feeling I Loved You

Forgive me for feeling I loved you

When my heart it was not free

I thus cannot give fully to you

In return love you gave unto me

I'll try to in ways make you happy

As we traverse or meet everyday

But I can't stay with you Love eternal

For the full hours of any long day

I must travel as I'll always wander

Like the wind, the time or the tide

I go or I come but I can't linger

I'm so sorry when I leave your side

Yet even the seasons all change

So why not the tide and the time

That's why I believe we'll exchange yet

Some love and some life sometime

One day the sun will shine brightly

And the cold wintry winds will not blow

We'll spend together our days and nightly

You'll ne'er again dear see me go

My life now is an empty retreat

Where for the times past I must pay

'Til forever we'll live love so sweet

When my prison of life goes away

The Will To Live...

He wavered for awhile
Tottered and swaggering fell
His unstable legs no longer
Would lend support his body to
The good Earth it rushed upwards
His face to meet and then
He laughed even as he lay there
Sprawled face-down upon the floor
For his was time and youth
This short walk but his first steps
Along paths that he must cross
As into life from infant child
To manhood he would grow
Each fall in weakness he
New strength would gain therefrom
Each dirtied face assuring
His sought goal would yet be found
For life'd made him a bargain
To stay his tottered swayings
Send support his weak legs to
If he but took the time to grow
And he did and entered boyhood
And he grew fast up and strong
Lending ears to words of wisdom
Lending eyes to right and wrong

Lending heart to joyful living
Friend he of the weak and strong
He wavered for awhile
Tottered and swaggering fell
His unstable legs no longer
Would lend support his body to
The wet muddy Earth rushed upwards
His face to meet and then
The bullets whistled as he lay there
All around lay dead his friends
For this was war and killing
This his duty he was told
To first kill all the enemy
For his country it's his goal
Then when last the guns are silent
And if return home safe you be
For your lost of legs in battle
Two firm sticks we'll give to thee
And he fought the battle bravely
But fought not the loss he had
Closed ears to words of wisdom
Closed eyes to right and wrong
Closed heart to joyful living
Friend no more of weak or strong

He wavered for awhile
Tottered and swaggering fell

His unstable stumps no longer
Would lend support his body to

And the gutters they rushed upwards
His worn distorted face to meet
As alone he lay forgotten
His bottle where once were his feet
Just a derelict of humanity
One who'd come the living route
To find there but exists still
One cold and fact-filled truth
We can be that which we want to
If our lives we take in hand
Be we infant child, healthy youth
Or poor drunk and crippled man
Life gives us its directions
But 'tis we who then must choose
To stay down once we've fallen
Or fates handouts to refuse
Then he fought the bottle bravely
And forgot the loss he had
Called deaf ears to words of wisdom
Showed blind eyes the right and wrong
Gave cold hearts a joyful living
Examples set for weak and strong
And his name lives on forever
He who thru his weakness became strong...

Oh Dreams Oh Dreams...

Last night I dreamed that you were here beside me
And in my arms warm your willing body lay
I dreamed I held you close and softly loved you
I dreamed our dark night turned into brightest day

Last night I dreamed your lips on mine did linger
Your heart beat soft and warm against my own
I dreamed things were the way we'd hoped them
I dreamed I heard you say "Love I've come home"

The flowers blossomed on the shrubs like springtime
The birds sang sweet above the snow-capped trees
The chills of winter gave way to warmth of summer
As I dreamed so real you lay here near to me

I dreamed of you last night but I awakened
I left my world of dreams as night went by
I awoke again alone without you with me
But memories of you in dreams will get me by

No tears I shed when I did full awaken
For they would serve I'm sure to only fill
My heart which longs for you with hurtful aching
My doubts to renew and my sweet dream to kill

Last night again in dreams you lay beside me
To me no closer could reality rest
I taste your lips I smell your woman's fragrance
I feel your welcome warmth against my chest

Oh dreams oh dreams purveyor you of feelings
Do you just reflect or are your reflections real
Let me not again awake with arms so empty
Having dreamt of home I yet can lingering feel

Last night I dreamed that you were here beside me
And in my arms warm your willing body lay
I dreamed I held you close and softly loved you
I dreamed our dark night turned into brightest day

But I awoke...
alone

A virgin is a woman who expects a man
to sign a blank paper before she prints
a lifetime marriage contract thereon

For A Dear Friend

Loneliness is no respecter
of age, beauty, station nor person
and it visits upon us all
paving a path for us
to fall into or one to follow out
towards some other lonely being
who too lives and lies
hidden behind some mask
of beauty, age, sickness,
riches or poverty
only shielded by that mask
that fully protects
recognition of them
from those who
have never truly known
the pains and emptiness
of true LONESOMENESS...

D.N.C. 24-6-89

Strange;

Most "bad" women are good yet
still few good women are bad if tried

If You Would But Treat Me Equal

Once I was young and healthy
And your battles I did fight
Then me upon a pedestal you placed
Now that I lay a-wounded
With my youthful movements stilled
You look with brief pity on my face
You see not me the living yet
The brain the will the soul
Which strives each day to sustain dignity
I beg not for your pity
I ask not for your gold
Understanding's all I ask that you give me
For tho I am a-wounded
And my strength of youth it fails
If you but treat me equal
I can live thru all my pains

In health and bodily beauty
I stayed close by your side
Your children I did bare you
Proud was I your blushing bride

Then as fate moved it happened
That my youth and body died
My outward shell 'came shambles
Tho I changed was not inside
But rejected and left lonely
Less than human me you see
Looked upon now just with pity
One you once loved open free
Me who now by sickness taken
'Til my youth and beauty failed
If you but treat me equal
I can live thru all my pains

Born to life by fate dejected
Slow in walk and slow in speech
Movements jerky and restricted
Short in stature short in reach
Looking not like many others
Hidden long me you did keep
Thoughtless of my many talents
Chained and waiting out to leap
Yet my brain it gave you healings
And my voice it gave you song
Books filled I with my writings
Which shall live on when I'm gone

For tho I was born afflicted
And youthful strength had none to fail
If you but treat me equal
I can live thru all my pains

Unto each of us is given
Talents hidden deep within
Which live on and on unchanging
Without regard to what has been
If in accident or turmoil
If in sickness or by fate
This our shell is somewhat damaged
Still inside these talents wait
Give a chance us to show it
Stay your pity and your sighs
For each loss we've but grown stronger
Still have dignity please realize
So tho I may be different
Tho my bodily strength doth fail
If you but treat me equal
We can live as humans just the same

An erection is the only commodity whose
supply is always equal only to its demand

> "A man is only as tall as the amount
> of conformity he refuses to accept"

Blood Of Innocents Cry

From deep beneath Afric's soil

The blood of innocent ages cry

Their tears bring out anew the toil

Falling on parched Earth they sigh

And the gaunt and empty faces

O'er the skeletal body frames

With sunken eyes in socketed places

Gaze at the dying with lost names

Knowing well tomorrows morning

Or mayhap this set of Sun

Their light moving back burden

Will become but yet another one

As the milk-less breasts of mothers

Suckle blood to their dying child

While on the fly-lined thirsting mouth

Deaths shadow faints a smile

The bones with skin but covered

No strength more to travel holds

Yet they drag themselves for miles

Hopeful aid tomorrow will unfold

Alas each new days beginning

But re-echoes what has been

And the famine line in quest for food

Like its victims grows more thin

And deep beneath Afric's soil

The blood of innocent ages cry

Will their pleas fall e'er on deafened ears

Like throughout centuries all gone by

From deep beneath Africa's soil ??

Disc23-1 - 042685

Clouds are to the sky

like women to millionaires

both slipping about

in silent beauty beneath

A Fact Of Justice...

Daddy why do people fight

My little boy said to me

Not conscious of the difference yet

Of the two men he could see

Daddy why do people hate

And speak in angry shout

And why is the man taking a gun

And shooting all about

Daddy what are police for

Do they only protect the one

Why did they shoot that poor old man

As he lay upon the ground

And Daddy why is it that they

These people all around

Walking off as if they cannot see

The man bleeding on the ground

Oh Daddy here comes an ambulance

It stops but now goes by

Why didn't it stop and help the man

Daddy I think he's gonna die

Please Daddy let me go and ask

If I can help somehow

There's only the lone policeman left

Standing proudly by him now
Daddy what was that he said
About you niggers and you Blacks
Did we do or say something wrong
That would cause him to us attack
Daddy look the man looks just like us
Black skin and blood so red
We can help him Daddy sure we can
"It's no use son the man is dead,
He's dead because the other man
The one that drove away
Was white and you have seen here son
The justice of white law today
You've seen the reach of centuries four
O'er which we Blacks have slaved
Just take another poor Black life
'Cause equality free he craved.

Freedom of speech extends up to
but does not include
valid testimony in many cases

> "For... it's not the outward looks of the mold
> which concerns the Master Craftsman
> but rather its inner beauty which will show
> itself fully in each casting"

The Swimming Pool

Today I watched a child of two

Swim across a swimming pool of water

Could you? Would you? Did you?

Didn't you? See it too... ??

Now today is long away and gone

Tomorrow has become yesterday

And I sit and watch a lonely child

Sitting off alone, afraid of that pool of water

Today in a park a laughing child of two

Was thrown into a swimming pool of water

A joy of childhood has been lost

Like dirt away too by that pool of water

And fear and anger sits instead

In that swimming pool of cool water

Today a parent sat and watched

As the other pushed the child into the water

An infant has been again abused

By force into that pool of water

And parents no fault here have seen

As they laughed at this child's disaster

Today a child of two cried out NO, NO

As it was thrown deep into a pool of water

Now years have passed gone by the way

No one recalls that pool filled up with water

Except the child still traumatized

Still in fear of a pool of water

And today I still tremble as I swim and as

I, today I watch a child of two

Scream and swim in panic to cross that water

Today I watch a child of two

Was it YOUR infant son or daughter?

The Quest of a Harmonious existence

is Scorpio's most elusive goal.

As I Stood There At The Trial

As I stood there at the trial
Feeling all alone and lost
As I heard the Judge say
You'll pay for what you've done
In that my weakest moment
When all my hopes were gone
I remembered God the Father and the Son

I remembered, I remembered, I remembered
Hearing glorious things they'd done
Tho my life will soon be over
And my time will all be past
I've found strength in the Father and the Son

I have lived a life so worldly
So careless and so free
Contented in the pleasures of my sins
I had thought my past life would never come undone
Then I remembered God the Father and the Son

I had lived for God before and had prospered for a time
But my roots on shallow ground did grow
And soon pleasures of the night life
Did beckon unto me
And in my weakness I did slowly to them go

Now the pleasures have turned sorrows
And at my trial I do stand
Accused of the awful things I've done
But I have deep consolation
Tho my Earthly hope is past
There's forgiveness in the Father and the Son

Infidelity is like eating at a restaurant while one
leaves good paid for food spoiling at home

Appreciation

Lady -- Both your brains
and feelings are hidden
within your body
Therefore
Please don't expect me
to appreciate
what you have hidden away
until I have
fully appreciated
that which you have
for me to feast
mine eyes upon

Me Alone

Anything, anywhere, anytime,

Alone

At home at work at play

In hill or dale

In park or trees

In Winter, Summer, Fall or Spring

Anywhere, anytime, anything

Alone

Without a thought a word

A whisper or a sound

With birds sweetly chirping

'Mongst Autumns rustling leaves

Above the slowly moving stream

Anytime, anything, anywhere,

Alone

Even strolling by restrictive

'Lectric fence

Or listening to the auto cars

Upon the long highways

Or the lone plane talking to itself

Anything, anywhere, anytime,

Alone

My thoughts are mine and free

I walk or run

Or stop and ponder

As thru life I move along

Anything,

anywhere,

anytime,

anyone,

ME

When years and time itself rolls by

-- the written word --

love and music alone remains unchanged

This Life To End

Be wary, you sweet, brown-skinned man --
Be wary, for this young creature
who has captured your heart is deceiving.
Be wary of the grey eyes
that look at you adoringly,
for they're cold and cutting.
Be wary of the lips
so full and red and tempting,
for their taste is momentarily sweet,
and will leave after the kiss, a bitter taste;
after the smile, an emptiness.
Be wary of the voice
so soft and seductive,
for the honey turns to vinegar
at the turn of a head.
Be wary of the breasts
that draw you near,
for unlike the mothers' nursing babe,
you won't be satisfied.
Be wary of the heart
that beats faster when you're near,
for it will only break yours
when you've surrendered all.
Be wary of the hands
that caress so gently and expertly,
for their mission is destruction,
as only hands can.

Be wary of the warm wet place
that men have fought and died for
to find their pleasure in;
for it's a trap, stronger than a bear's,
and you'll never be free
of its jaws once in.
Be wary of the legs and feet
that run to greet you warmly,
for they'll run harder
the other way
when they tire of you.
Be wary of the body
that responds so emphatically
with this erotic coupling of youth,
for as it wraps around you in passion,
it is your prison.
Yes, be wary of all these things,
my love, for they belong to me,
and I am void of feelings.
It matters not who receives
my poisoned darts of sweet words
that spread like cancer
to destroy the body and soul.
Be wary, you sweet brown-skinned man,
for I am your demise.
I make men wish life to end,
even that they'd never been born.

"Language"

Though fast so fast the horsemen ride

Though I be heir to Caymans throne

I 'light and press my ear unto the ground

That I might hear and here understand

E'er less I err like common man

Then by my folly this battle lose.

Then onwards lead, I set a pace

No lead in shot, nor time to waste

The battle reed in song I read

The weather red in sky I read above

While I unto the battle ride

There to too defend my Island's pride

Aye, I, my eye with dusty pain

Recall the Inn wherein I'd rest

From sword and shield and battle shot

Bathe in a bath of sunlight's gleam

Which shone from high through windows pane

Erase from my mind, this battle mine

But alas around my waist

Life's waste is hung

And battle weary draws me down

Yet I still live must live again

Carry on the fight to which I ride

Carry on 'til death my country's pride.

June 1989 QPR

If You Believe That

If you believe that

-- WELL --

I've got some

oceanfront property in old Nevada

A bridge or two that'll sound

just right with your name

A beautiful virgin daughter

of 35 in southern California

And a foolproof plan to bring you

instant fortune and fame

Be All You Want To Be

In this world and life of love
You can be anything you want to be
You can be the best you want to be
You can be better than the rest
If... you really want to...
There are three secrets to this success
Given by the young to the old
In wordless example as we watch them grow
To walk because they see others doing so
To walk because they also want to
To walk because they believe they can
So too does a duckling swim and a sparrow fly
You can be all you want to be...
By one : using books or films or instructional example
two : applying that gained from one
three : by practice of one and two
With belief that you can be,
whatever you want to be
And thereby you will be the best at whatever
You desire most to excel in your life...
You own the universe because it is within you
You rule the world because you are in it
Fulfill your life by wanting, believing
And accepting nothing less than being the best...
It is in you, you control it.
Go now and make it YOURS

200604 DC

About The Author:

Dudley Noel Christian, or "Chris" as he prefers to be called, was born in Trinidad on November 15, 1944. Within his first year on this planet, he was moved to his father's homeland, Grand Cayman. He schooled there, along with his siblings of two brothers and four sisters. As he grew older, he gradually learned that his proud ancestry had the adversity of being caught up into slavery.

At 16, Chris took to the sea, which furthered his education in the psychological aspects of mankind, which was so different (and sometimes brutally so) from the mentality of the islanders, which he had been so comfortable with. At 19, he returned home to study various career choices, created a small business, and built his own home. At 23, he travelled to Canada, intent on exploring possibilities of immigrating there.

Leaving a son behind, when his girlfriend refused to leave Cayman, Chris immigrated to Canada. Soon he met Grace, a librarian, and of Polish descent, whom he married and had two children with. This alliance was in the early days of multicultural relationships and the two were a team combating a lifetime of racial injustice.

Chris obtained employment with BC Ferries, enjoyed working on these ships and on the waters. He slowly worked his way up, battling ethnological discrimination at every step, from the catering department and into the engine room. In spite of the difficulties and conflicts, he managed with pride, to reach the day he earned his final ticket and became the first black Chief Engineer with this company.

After 30 years of marriage, he lost his wife to cancer in 1997. He struggled to deal with this devastation, until Marilyn came along, his second chance for happiness. In 1998, he married this postal worker, who was proud of her Ukrainian heritage, and possessed skills for whatever project she put her mind to.

Marilyn, with her interest in genealogy, attempted to document a Christian family tree, running into a multitude of problems in her searches of records about his slave ancestry. Although some of this family tree is word of mouth information passed down from older relatives, she has learned that Chris is a descendant of Fletcher Christian, on his paternal line, and related to Napoleon's officer Admiral Gantaume, on his maternal line. Chris always knew that that he is a grandson of Carib & Arawack Indians and of Los Bravos, the very proud runaway slaves.

Chris retired as a marine engineer in 2004 and five years later, Marilyn retired as well. The two pensioners enjoy extensive travelling abroad, cruising and RVing the countryside in their motorhome. When they are not travelling, they implemented a system to compile his lifetime collection of poetry and other literary compositions into books.

Take the time to listen to the anecdotes passed down into these books as a result of a lifetime of living in many corners...

Other Collections by This Author:

A Poet's Ebb And Flow

... and Touches Of Nature

In The Middle of Believe There's A Lie

Inside A Heart

Judge Me Not Without A Trial

Legends, Lives & Loves Along the Inside Passage

Love... Life's Illusive Zenith

Love's Reflections

Love's Refuge and Sonnets

Only Children Of The Universe Are We

Step Scenes Of Life

~ ~

For more information go to:

w w w . d n c s i t e . c a

~ ~